Original title:
The Poetry of Potted Plants

Copyright © 2025 Creative Arts Management OÜ
All rights reserved.

Author: Cameron Blair
ISBN HARDBACK: 978-1-80581-898-4
ISBN PAPERBACK: 978-1-80581-425-2
ISBN EBOOK: 978-1-80581-898-4

Elegy for an Eclipsed Flower

In a pot dull and gray, she sat,
Wondering why her friends go flat.
Her blooms were bright, full of cheer,
Yet the sun played hide and seek all year.

A little sprout whispered soft jokes,
While her leaves curled up like croaking folks.
She sighed as she watched the moon take flight,
Her petals drooped—where's the sunlight?

The Drumbeat of Dirt

Oh, the rhythm of soil, so lively, so bold,
Rattling worms tell stories of old.
Each flash of a trowel, such a raucous sound,
Dancing roots beneath, jiving underground.

The seeds perform a tap dance, quite spry,
Twisting and turning, oh my, oh my!
Their tiny percussion, a tuneful delight,
Curious critters groove through the night.

Rhythm of the Rainwater

Pitter-patter drops from clouds so keen,
Make every leaf glisten, oh what a scene!
The plants sway gently, a whimsical jig,
While snails waltz along, oh so big!

A splashy concert as puddles form,
To dapple the ground, a water-filled norm.
They sip with a sigh, 'Ah, sweet serenade!'
Chatting 'til sunbeams come to invade.

Canvas of Colors: A Plant's Tale

A canvas bright, all shades of green,
With reds and yellows, a gardener's dream.
Petunias giggle in the summer's gleam,
While ferns plot colors—a wily scheme.

Bouncing pots with personalities bound,
Chattering leaves in a swirling sound.
A riot of hues, each brushstroke alive,
In the gallery of nature, they all thrive.

Stanzas in the Sunlight

In the corner, basking bright,
Little greens reach for the light.
A fern whispers jokes, oh so sly,
While potting soil laughs, oh my!

A succulent styles its little hair,
Confident blooms, beyond compare.
Cactus giggles in stiff, prickly glee,
While daisies dance, wild and free!

The basil dreams of pasta nights,
Chives sing songs of kitchen fights.
All together, a raucous crew,
In their sunny spot, with skies so blue!

When evening falls and shadows creep,
They all share secrets, laughter deep.
Potted pals in vibrant bloom,
Creating mischief in every room!

The Secret Life of Sedge

In the shade, a sedge does plot,
Scheming ways to take a shot.
With whispers sweet, it paints a scene,
A destiny beyond routine.

Worms parade like little jesters,
Underneath the leaf-born festers.
Together they conspire and scheme,
While the soil smiles, living the dream!

Shh! Don't tell the daffodils,
Sedge plans a heist for garden thrills.
With roots as stealthy as a cat,
Stealing the spotlight, imagine that!

And when the sun begins to fade,
The secret life begins to trade.
Their jokes in shadows twist and twine,
In the garden world, all is divine!

Rhyme of the Rooted

Rooted deep in soil and stone,
Each plant has quirks, each has its tone.
A vine teased a nearby tree,
"Grow taller, buddy! Come laugh with me!"

Petunias puff with pride up high,
While peppers peek and wonder why.
"Who's the fairest?" asks the thyme,
"Let's have a contest, it'll be sublime!"

The daisies romp, a flowery show,
"Pick us, pick us!" they chirp in tow.
With playful hearts, they spin and sway,
In the garden dance, they play all day!

But when the moonlight starts to gleam,
Secrets shared spill like cream.
Oh, the rhymes that roots can weave,
In the soil where they never leave!

Serenade for the Stalwart Cactus

Oh, stalwart friend with spines so proud,
You stand so still beneath the cloud.
While others wilt in summer heat,
You strut your stuff with prickly beat!

A serenade sung soft and low,
To you, dear cactus, we give a show.
"Don't take life too serious, dear,"
You say, as laughter starts to steer!

Flowers bloom atop your crown,
A royal gift, the talk of town.
You grin with glee, though just a tease,
A hiding warmth in desert breeze!

As friends gather, a laughter spree,
You regale tales of roots so free.
In the garden, a curious sight,
A stalwart spirit shining bright!

Rooted in Serenity

In a pot so snug and round,
A leafy friend can often be found.
With dirt on their face, they beam with glee,
Sharing secrets, just them and me.

Water splashes, but they never mind,
In their stillness, joy you'll find.
With roots that wiggle, they're having a blast,
In this little home, time moves fast.

Petal Ponderings

Petals rustle in gentle air,
They whisper secrets without a care.
Oh, what's a flower's favorite jest?
To bloom too late is a flower's quest!

In sunshine, they dance like they've won a prize,
While sneaky ants try to steal their ties.
With that bright smile, they have no fear,
For life in a pot means party time, my dear!

Sheltered Splendor

Underneath a canopy so vast,
Little pots hold stories from the past.
A cactus grins, full of prickly cheer,
While the daisy dreams of being a deer.

In the rain, they giggle, jump and sway,
Splashing puddles all across their day.
With soil hugs and gentle sun,
They know life's a game, and it's all just fun!

Fragmented Sunlight

Sunlight dances on leaves so bright,
Each ray a brush painting pure delight.
They've got the wisdom of ages unfurled,
In pots, they plot to take over the world!

A peeking snail gives a comic view,
While a sleepy fern dreams of morning dew.
With every sprout, laughter takes flight,
In this quirky garden, all feels right.

Cradled in Clay

In a pot so round and stout,
A cactus danced, with a goofy pout.
It jiggled in the sun's sweet glow,
Saying, 'Plant me deeper, let's go slow!'

The herbs were busy, plotting schemes,
A basil shared its wildest dreams.
'What if we danced?' the mint did yell,
'Then let's toast to wishes, what a swell!'

The fern was flipping through the day,
A somersault in breezy play.
With fronds like arms, it waved with glee,
'Oh, swing by later, sip some tea!'

At night they snickered, roots entwined,
Laughter bubbled, all aligned.
In their earthy world, so bright and gay,
They'd pot-a-luck till another day.

The Artistry of Earth

A sunflower wore a silly grin,
With a floppy hat, it let the fun begin.
'Look at me! I'm the tallest here!
Gotta stretch it out, to see so clear!'

The violets chuckled, in their hues,
'We're the artists; we're the muse!'
With petals wide, they painted bright,
While snails played tag under soft moonlight.

A pot-bellied tulip stood with pride,
'The more the pot, the better I stride!'
In the garden, tales grew tall,
Of plants who boasted, and those who'd fall.

While shadows danced and crickets sang,
The garden giggled, such joyous clang.
Nature laughed, in its earthy birth,
Finding joy in the artistry of earth.

Blossoms in the Mist

In morning mist, a daisy grinned,
'Today I'll spin; let's see who'll win!'
With petals twirling in fresh, clean air,
It tossed its pollen without a care.

A cheeky geranium joined the fun,
Said, 'I bet you can't outshine the sun!'
But as it blushes in rosy red,
The sun just winked, 'You're cute,' it said.

Beneath the leaves, the potting soil,
Held secrets of laughter, endless toil.
They whispered jokes of dirt and grime,
While seedlings plotted their dance in time.

As shadows lingered and day did fade,
Each plant agreed, their joy wouldn't trade.
In every bloom amidst the twist,
They found their glee in blossoms, kissed.

Treasures in the Mud

In the garden, roots entwine,
Earthy treasures you can't find.
A worm sings songs quite absurd,
While the soil dances, so unheard.

Potting mix, a sticky spree,
A tiny frog leaps joyfully.
With trowel in hand, I dig and weave,
My plants just giggle, I believe.

Sunflowers wear sunglasses bright,
Cacti sport a ball of light.
A daisy tells a punny tale,
While ivy climbs a leafy trail.

So come and join this garden fun,
Where potted pals play in the sun.
With every sprout, there's laughter near,
And muddy hands bring joy and cheer.

Portrait of a Petal

A petal struck a pose so grand,
With hues so bright, it took a stand.
Said, "Take my picture, don't delay,
I'm the star, come on, let's play!"

The daffodils were feeling bold,
With stories of glory yet untold.
While violets whispered to the breeze,
"Pose us right, if you please!"

Succulents smirked, quite plump and round,
"Check our angles, we're highly renowned!"
The orchid struck a diva's pose,
With petals flared, and nose in rows.

So snap a pic in this floral spree,
Each plant is art, can't you see?
In this gallery, all things bloom,
With laughter echoing through the room.

Echoes of Existence

In a pot, the silence hums,
As each sprout sighs, the tension comes.
The sage whispers to the thyme,
"Let's share secrets, it'll be sublime."

A cactus chuckles with its spikes,
"Do come closer, I'm full of gripes!"
The fern just giggles, gently swaying,
While the basil dreams of gourmet playing.

The chirping birds tune in to chat,
While gossipy plants share where they're at.
"Could we grow taller?" one petunia cried,
"Or just be proud of this leafy ride?"

As pots together share their fate,
With whispers that can make you wait.
A symphony within each sprout,
Echoing laughter, there's never doubt.

Herbal Harmonies

Mint sings sweetly from its pot,
Basil joins in, what a hot shot!
Cilantro chimed in with a twist,
"Oregano, don't let dreams be missed!"

Thyme keeps time like a cozy clock,
While rosemary struts in a herb-y frock.
Parsley giggles, curls on a spree,
As chives pass jokes so expertly!

In the kitchen, they dance with glee,
Creating dishes, a taste jubilee.
With every chop, they sing and sway,
In this fragrant, fun ballet!

So here we hum, the herbs unite,
In pot and pan, it's pure delight.
A melody stirred in flavors fine,
Herbal harmonies, so divine!

Sunlight Serenade

In the morning light they sway,
Joking under sun's warm ray.
Chasing shadows, playing tag,
Potted friends will never lag.

One says, "I feel so spry!"
Another laughs, "Let's reach for the sky!"
They drink the sun like lemonade,
With every giggle, plans are made.

Leaves in Conversation

Two leaves gossip, oh so sly,
"Did you see the cat pass by?"
"Grown-ups fuss, and overhead,
We just dance, without a thread."

One leaf flutters, "What a breeze!
Feeling fancy, look at me tease!"
With every chirp, they grow more bold,
Sharing secrets, stories told.

Blossoms of Resilience

A bloom appears, with cheeky flair,
Says, "I'll grow, just you beware!"
In spite of storms, it stands up high,
With petals bright against the sky.

"Watch me blossom, can't you see?
I'm tougher than a burrito spree!"
Each petal laughing with delight,
Ready to dance, through day and night.

Silent Growth

Roots beneath, they plot and scheme,
"Let's grow taller, what a dream!"
They chuckle low, in earthy talk,
While above, the daisies mock.

Slow and steady, in a race,
"I'll outgrow you, just find your place!"
In gentle silence, life takes hold,
Potted pals are brave and bold.

Green Verses in Clay

In a pot so small and round,
My basil dreams it wears a crown.
But twenty leaves and still no fame,
It's sad to see it play this game.

A cactus jokes, so sharp and bright,
"I'm prickly yet, but that's alright!"
With every poke, it stands so proud,
A spiky knight amidst the crowd.

A leafy friend in mossy shade,
Pretending it's a grand parade.
"Just one more sip!" the fern insists,
With water dancing on its mist.

While violets sigh and gossip low,
"Do you think the sun's in love? Oh no!"
With petals bright, they laugh and tease,
Creating joy, as if on breeze.

Whispers of Ferns

In corners dark, the ferns do scheme,
"Let's throw a shade and start a dream!"
With fronds that flutter like a fan,
They plan a party—oh, how grand!

A lonesome leaf begins to croon,
"I'll sway near windows, make 'em swoon!"
Together they are quite a sight,
A leafy laughter, day and night.

They whisper secrets to the dust,
"Can you believe the sunlight's lust?"
While spiders weave a dance so fine,
A tango mixed with webs and twine.

And if you think that plants can't play,
Just watch them spin a leafy ballet!
Oh, those shy greens, in pot and clay,
Turn every frown to bright display.

Ode to the Succulent

The succulent sits, all cool and sly,
"Too much water? Oh me, oh my!"
A thirsty voice it likes to greet,
"When dry is comfy, that's my treat!"

With plumpness grand, it shares a wink,
"Who needs the rain? I'm bright, don't blink!"
In shades of green and pink it glows,
A pleasant joke that nobody knows.

Cacti sing of lonely woes,
"Too prickly sharp, nobody knows!"
Yet they convene with laughter round,
In crumbling soil, fun's surely found.

While generations come and go,
The plant parade puts on a show!
For in the pots, the laughter hums,
Creating joy—just wait for sun!

Sonnets from the Soil

In soil deep, a mystery stirs,
"Watch out for weeds!" the garden whirs.
While daisies toss their petals bright,
Mars appears in the garden's light.

The kale, it dreams of greener days,
While dandelions prance with praise.
"Pull me up! I'm still in my prime!"
And yet those greens don't care for crime.

The herbs like to play dress-up grand,
"Just sprinkle me; my growth is planned!"
With spicy flair and scents so neat,
They dance their way to every feast.

In pots or rows, the laughter spills,
A symphony of joyful thrills.
So come and join this leafy jest,
For in the garden, life's the best!

Verses from the Vine

In a pot, a grape holds court,
Stubborn and spry, dreams are fought.
Each sunbeam a chance, it sways,
Whispering secrets of sunny days.

Basil sings of Italian nights,
While mint throws shade in leafy fights.
Tomato blushing, green with pride,
Cracks a joke at the veggie side.

Cactus, prickly, tells tall tales,
Of desert quests and rainstorm gales.
A twist of fate, he's in a jam,
Surrounded by friends—beets and ham!

In this garden stage, they play alive,
Each petal and leaf putting on a jive.
So grab your pot and join the fun,
With laughter and joy, our work is done!

Prologue in Petals

Daisies giggle, bright and small,
Inviting all to the garden ball.
Butterflies flutter, dashing in,
With a tiny zap, the pranks begin.

Ferns do a dance but twist and tangle,
A snooty rose gives a sarcastic jangle.
Laughter erupts from the daisies' crew,
As the tulip jokes, "What's red and blue?"

Pansies pose like models in bloom,
While violets scheme to take the room.
"Watch my best side!" they all declare,
But weeds just snicker; "You're beyond repair!"

As the sun sets, the laughter grows,
Each petal a tale, each leaf a prose.
In this pot, strange friendships bloom,
In a garden where joy is always in full room!

Epiphany of the Evergreen

Pines speak softly, with needles sharp,
In the corner, a gnome plays a harp.
Firs chime in with tales of snow,
"Evergreen? More like ever-flow!"

Spruces forgo the winter chill,
Trading insulted wit with will.
"Yo, Cedar, don't be so stuck up,
Ever thought of letting your needles drop?"

Bamboo bursts in, tall with grace,
Swaying gently, a green embrace.
"Don't worry boys, I'm here to stay,
Flexibility is my middle name, I say!"

In this green family, laughter reigns,
Even the moss returns with gains.
Embrace the quirks, let friendship fray,
As the evergreens paint the world their way!

Haiku of Healing Herbs

Mint whispers secrets,
Bringing calm in every sip,
The world slows down, hush.

Sage shrugs off the past,
"Regrets? I perfume the air,
Move on, lovely friend."

Thyme tickles the tongue,
A playful jest in each pot,
Laughter fills the stew.

Chives throw a party,
A gathering of spice and zest,
In every bite, cheer!

Nature's Gentle Presence

In a corner sits a fern,
Waving like it's got a turn.
A cactus claims it's very tough,
But watch out, it can get quite gruff!

The violets sing a silly song,
While busy bees buzz all day long.
A sprout declares, 'I am the king!'
But can't quite reach the bird that sings.

The succulents take selfies too,
For Instagram, they've got a crew.
A bonsai's wisdom, sadly small,
Says, "Meditation's worth it all!"

Together they make quite a sight,
A leafy crew, from morn till night.
With every petal, sprout, and stem,
They laugh and dance—oh, what a gem!

Flora and Fauna Dialogues

A daisy asked a neighbor vine,
"Why do you twist and try to climb?"
The vine replied, with great delight,
"Because it's fun to reach new height!"

A snappy tulip snorts with glee,
"I'm the brightest—can't you see?"
But nearby, a dandelion grins,
"Yet I'm the one who always wins!"

In pots, they gossip all day long,
While earthworms hum a funny song.
Floors of greens in cheerful array,
Keep drabness far and out of play!

"Oh sprout, you're so naive," they tease,
As sunlight dances through the leaves.
In leafy laughter, wisdom thrives,
These porch pals know how joy survives.

A Tapestry of Greens

In a patch of dirt, a radish dreams,
Hoping for happy salad screams.
A basil whispers secrets bold,
"Confessions of a spice, I'm told!"

Pansies gossip, colors bright,
Comparing shades, they find delight.
A creeping thyme struts with flair,
"Watch me grow, if you dare!"

A curious sprout stretched out too wide,
Lands in quicksand, oh what a ride!
"It's all good," says a rooted sage,
"Adventure lives at every age!"

Together they form a crazy crew,
A garden party, just for you.
With every rustle, chirp, and cheer,
This leafy gathering draws us near!

Whispers in the Clay

In the soil, where secrets dwell,
Plants convene, all is swell.
A shy sprout mumbles 'what's the fuss?'
While elders grin and say "Don't rush!"

A sunflower yawns, looking tall,
"I hear the gossip, it's a ball!"
With petals waving, it prepares,
To spill the tea on thorns and lairs.

A chatty herb starts a debate,
"Who's the most stylish of the great?"
While moss giggles, rolling in green,
It claims the title, "Best unseen!"

From pot to pot, the laughter flies,
Tiny leaves with big surprise.
So next time when you look and play,
Remember they have much to say!

Fragrant Chronicles

In corners the herbs whisper and tease,
Chives giggle, and basil rides the breeze.
Mint sips tea with a leafy grin,
While rosemary plots its secret win.

Cacti brag of their prickly charm,
Insisting they don't require a farm.
Succulents lounge in their sunny spots,
Throwing shade at those with too many pots.

A fern frond flirts with the sunlight glow,
Claiming it knows more than the rest can show.
With tales of drought and a vacation,
It laughs at those in constant agitation.

So here they stand, in their green parade,
Each pot a stage, a playful charade.
As we water, they respond with cheer,
Telling stories of growth we want to hear.

Leafy Legacies

The houseplant club meets at dawn's first light,
With gossiping leaves that get quite a fright.
A spider plant stated it's the best in town,
While snake plants smirk, wearing their green crown.

Peace lilies dance to a gentle tune,
While pothos sigh under the bright full moon.
Each pot a throne; the chatter won't cease,
As ferns debate which is the greatest piece.

Orchids prance with petals so grand,
Trying hard to make their demands.
With blooms as jokes, they wink and sway,
As the leaves laugh, saying, "We're here to stay!"

So lift your mug and toast to the crew,
In our humble homes, they flourish anew.
These leafy legends share a hearty cheer,
With roots grounded deep, we hold them dear.

The Stillness of Growth

In the quiet of soil, a seed starts to yawn,
Stretching its arms as it greets the dawn.
With dreams of reaching the sky so high,
    It giggles at clouds that drift by.

A timid sprout peeks from beneath the earth,
Wondering what this whole thing is worth.
As it wiggles up, it can't help but pout,
"Why is everyone talking about chores like clout?"

With whispers of roots, they giggle and sway,
    Sharing secrets of sunshine and play.
In stillness, they know how laughter blooms,
Transforming the air, filling empty rooms.

Growth may be slow, but joy is the key,
These plants dream of heights we can't wait to see.
Laughter in pots is what we embrace,
As nature's humor thrives in this space.

Simple Wonders

A little pot sits, with dirt on its face,
"Just give me some sun, and I'll find my place!"
Succulent jokes on the windowsill,
Whispering softly, "Let's skip the thrill."

The violets chuckle, dressed all in shades,
Telling the daisies their art never fades.
While jade plants boast their emerald sheen,
Saying, "Watering's nice, but I'm still the queen."

A busy bee buzzes around the bloom,
While petunias gossip, "We've got the room!"
In simple wonders, their humor unfolds,
As each layered leaf has a story it holds.

So cherish the jokes that grow from the soil,
As plants weave their laughter, a spirit to toil.
With each little sprout, life brings a grin,
In our leafy companions, the joy begins.

Tiny Ecosystems

In my tiny pot, a jungle thrives,
A busy world where a cactus jives.
The fern tells jokes, the moss laughs loud,
While succulents strut, all hyped and proud.

On the sill, they dance, a leafy fling,
With roots so deep, they take to wing.
A playful breeze joins in their spree,
As daisies giggle, wild and free.

Each day a party, with soil as cake,
A muddy bash, for goodness' sake!
I sit and chuckle, my green friends tease,
In their little world, we do as we please.

Oh, to be a plant, what fun to be!
Life in ceramic, a potpourri!
Digging deep brought laughter anew,
In these tiny homes, joy always grew.

Petals in a Jar

A jar of petals, oh what a view,
With bright little blooms, I smile anew.
They gossip softly, whisper and sigh,
As I sit nearby, oh me, oh my!

A tulip winks, a daisy grins,
Their silly chatter makes my head spin.
In sunshine they bask, with colors so bright,
Beneath the jar's warmth, such pure delight.

When the breeze stirs, they sway and cheer,
Tiny shenanigans, no seedling fear!
Each petal a giggle, each stem a joke,
In this glassy realm, we all evoke.

So here I watch, enchanted and bright,
My floral friends in a splendid sight.
In this simple jar, joy's filled to the brim,
With petals dancing, life can't be dim!

Loam and Laughter

Buried in loam, the roots do play,
Where worms tell secrets and fungi sway.
A sprinkle of humor, a shovel of cheer,
Each scoop of dirt brings laughter near.

The malevolent weeds put on a show,
As dandelions giggle, putting on a glow.
Now here comes the sun, with a wink and a grin,
Because in this garden, all joy begins.

With tiny wheels spinning, the potters work,
Crafting the dirt with a mischievous quirks.
The laughter echoes, each pluck a delight,
In loamy chaos, hearts feel so light.

So let's dig deep, no need for a frown,
In this earthy world, joy wears a crown.
For every speck, a chuckle we share,
In loam and laughter, there's magic in air.

The Art of Stillness

In pots they ponder, the art of calm,
Sipping their sunlight, feeling the balm.
A cactus sits proud, with sharp little quips,
While the ferns tell tales of grandeur trips.

Oh, the stillness they master with such delight,
But dare tease a leaf? They'll spring up to fight!
In silence they bicker, in patience they bide,
While sipping the dew, with nature as guide.

When shadows stretch long, they share quiet laughs,
Discussing the merits of water and baths.
Each moment's a treasure, each breath a gift,
In this quiet patch, their spirits uplift.

So cherish the stillness, let laughter entwine,
In pots of green wonders, confusion aligns.
With every soft rustle, life's canvas unfolds,
In the art of stillness, the magic molds!

Fragmented Silences

In a pot sits a cactus quite prickly,
It stabs at my thoughts, oh so quickly.
Its silent demeanor, a curious sight,
Yet it tells me secrets deep in the night.

A fern near the window, swaying with glee,
Whispers sweet nothings, just to me.
The more I listen, the more I grin,
It offers up laughter – where have I been?

The herbs in the kitchen, a fragrant crew,
Basil and thyme, always something to brew.
They giggle and gossip, plot with their leaves,
While I just chuckle, oh what a tease!

Alone in my corner, I talk to a plant,
Why does it seem like it knows my chant?
Its green little face, a comical friend,
In potted conspiracy, we laugh until the end.

Time in the Terrarium

Inside this glass dome, time takes a stroll,
Mossy adventurers plotting a goal.
The soil is a stage, with actors so bold,
Ferns dance like they have stories untold.

Mushrooms peek out with a cheeky grin,
Eager to join in on the whimsy within.
Cacti look on, arms crossed in delight,
While snails move in slow-mo, what a sight!

A leaf in the corner, droopy yet wise,
Sighs like a scholar with half-opened eyes.
It rolls its green past like an old crone,
While guffaws of laughter make it feel at home.

The light filters in with a spot and a wink,
Gathering the plants for a pint and a drink.
Time in the terrarium, oh, what a blast,
A party with greens - forever a laugh that lasts!

Sprouts of Serenity

In my sunny window, a riot of green,
Potted companions, the funnies unseen.
They thrive and they chatter, oh what a scene,
Sprouts of serenity, living so keen.

An orchid demands just the right kind of light,
Pouting when she feels a shade is too tight.
Meanwhile, the chives laugh, bringing zest to the day,
While whispers of parsley sway wild and play!

Each tiny sprout has a joke on the side,
They plot in the soil, with laughter as pride.
A wild dandelion, a rogue in the mix,
Confuses the kittens with plant-based tricks.

In quirky arrangements, they sway with delight,
Making my home feel so warm and so bright.
Sprouts of serenity, charming and spry,
Who knew that my plants would make all spirits fly?

Earthy Epiphanies

In a started-up pot, a bean finds its glee,
Dreaming of climb walls, oh, how it wants to be free.
It wriggles and squirms, roots taking flight,
Metallic dreams under a bulb's glowing light.

A marigold muses, with petals like gold,
Tales of the garden, so brash and so bold.
Composting secrets from soil and from heart,
Wise words of the earth, what a glimmering art!

Green thumbs at work, concocting weird brews,
Mixing their potions while tracking the news.
Banter of blooms mingles with dirt so divine,
An earthy epiphany - laughter in line!

With every new sprout, there's a story to tell,
In jokes with the roots, we all do quite well.
Earthy epiphanies, sprouting delight,
Growing together, our friendship takes flight!

The Keeper of Green

In a pot sits my leafy friend,
With a smile that seems to blend.
A sprinkle of water, a dash of light,
He waves his leaves, what a sight!

Every morning, he greets the sun,
Whispering secrets, oh what fun!
The cat thinks he's a climbing toy,
A leafy target for feline joy!

A Mosaic of Life

A pot of joy, a mix of hues,
Succulents and ferns, sharing views.
Each leaf a story, each stem a tale,
With laughter growing, we cannot fail.

Oh, the cactus kept making jokes,
While the orchids laughed at the oak folks.
A gathering of greens, quite absurd,
Nature's laughter without a word!

Hidden Wonders in Pots

Underneath the soil, treasures hide,
A critter's party, growing wide!
A worm wearing glasses to read a book,
And a beetle dressed like a chef off the hook!

They share their tales when the night is near,
With moonlit giggles that only we hear.
Tap dancing roots, a wild ballet,
In this pot, surprises come out to play!

The Timeless Terrestrial

Time moves slowly for my potted crew,
A snail in a race, oh what a view!
The fern tells jokes, while the dirt takes bets,
Who wins, the snail? He's full of regrets!

With each new sprout comes a stand-up show,
They laugh at my gardening, say, 'Nice try, though!'
Each day a giggle wrapped in green bliss,
In this little jungle, who could resist?

Nature's Small Secrets

In the corner sits a cactus, proud and tall,
With spines so sharp, it's ready for a brawl.
Each morning it greets me with a cheeky grin,
Saying, 'Water me not, or you'll face my sin!'

A fern whispers tales of ancient rhymes,
Of dancing in the breeze during summer times.
Its leaves grow curly, like spaghetti in a cook,
'Be careful!' it warns, 'I might just take a look!'

Next door, a thyme has ambitions, oh so grand,
Dreaming of herbs mixing in a rock band.
But every time it plays, it's out of tune,
'Just call me Maestro!' it cries to the moon.

Oh, the secrets these pots hold, oh so bright,
With dreams of growing taller with all their might.
They spin their yarns on sunny windowsills,
In the world of greenery, it's laughter that thrills!

Threads of Nature

Tangled roots beneath, a gnome takes a nap,
Mossy and cozy, it's a mystical trap.
While daisies plot a party, with petals so fine,
They're sure to please with their flowery wine.

A spider spins webs, crafting artwork in haste,
'Look, it's a gallery!' the tulips all taste.
They quip and they giggle, they fill up the air,
'Let's host an exhibition of flowers so rare!'

One little succulent joins in the fun,
With stories of sunlight and warmth from the sun.
'I'm tough as nails,' it says with a wink,
'But fond of a party with a splash and a drink!'

So here in this pot, friendships bloom and grow,
Laughter and fun, as they steal the show.
Nature's threads weave a tale, a jolly affair,
With roots intertwined and smiles everywhere!

Gentle Green Chronicles

On a shelf sits a bamboo, tall and spry,
Flexing its leaves as if reaching for the sky.
'Just call me Sir Flex,' it claims with a cheer,
I do yoga each morning; come join me, my dear!'

The peace lily chuckles, wrapped in white hue,
'While you're all bending, I've got chores to do!
I clean all the air while you stretch to the sun,
With beauty and charm, I'll always have fun!'

A mischievous ivy climbs higher, it seems,
Creating a maze of nature's wild dreams.
'Try and catch me!' it dares with a laugh,
As it dances around like a playful giraffe.

So in pots so scattered, life winks and plays,
With gentle chronicles of sunny days.
Each leaf has a story, a giggle, a cheer,
In the world of green wonders, joy's always near!

Lifelines in Pottery

This little plant keeps a diary of hues,
Recording the stains of spilled coffee and blues.
It writes of the sunlight that tickles its face,
And of the long hours spent in special quiet space.

The basil argues back, with flair and with spice,
'Dear diary, I'm yummy; oh, isn't that nice?'
As it dreams of being a topping on pie,
Saying, 'Let's spice life up before we say goodbye!'

A little orchid struts, wearing purple so bold,
Snootily suggesting, 'I'm the queen of the fold!'
But when it rains, oh how it gets so shy,
'Cover me up, I'm too precious to dry!'

In this merry throng, each leaf has its tale,
From the tiny sprouts to those destined to sail.
Lifelines in pottery, a mix of the grand,
In the laughter of leaves, nature's humor is planned!

Dances in Decorative Planters

In pots of clay, with colors so bright,
The ferns do a jig, oh what a sight!
Succulents shimmy, all snug and neat,
While cacti prickle to the funky beat.

With each little leaf, they sway and bend,
Bouncing in rhythm, as friends so blend.
A dance-off ensues, oh what a thrill,
In this quirky realm, they strut at will.

Chlorophyll crowd goes wild with glee,
Critters stop by, say, "Can we join the spree?"
A garden soirée, with laughter galore,
Come join us, dear friend, don't be a bore!

With sunlight they twirl, in joy they bask,
Who knew a pot could be such a blast?
So grab a green buddy, it's time to groove,
In our dance party, let's make a move!

Garden of Words

In pots that speak, with leaves so spry,
A tale unfolds, as breezes sigh.
Each stem a sentence, bright and bold,
Whispers of wisdom, gently told.

Petunias murmur, their secrets shared,
While daisies giggle, showing they cared.
Oh, listen close, for you might just find,
A pun in the petals, oh so refined!

"Lettuce grow together," one flower said,
"While thyme helps us think," another one led.
In this patchwork plot of plant puns neat,
The garden blooms with laughter, sweet!

As bees buzz along, a chorus of cheer,
Nature's own jesters, drawing us near.
So in this bright plot, come sit for a while,
Join in the chatter and share a smile!

Whispers of Green

In corners dim, a jade plant chats,
About mysterious hats worn by cats.
The basil teases, "I smell very nice,"
While orchids practice their best sultry spice.

They giggle and gossip, with sprigs all around,
In the quiet corners, their voices abound.
"Do you think we're cute?" asks the shy little sprout,
"Oh, we're fab!" the big leaves shout, without doubt!

The mint chews gum, making quite the fuss,
"I'd wear shades too, if I were as lush!"
With petals a-twinkle in the soft light,
These whispers of green spark joy and delight.

So lend an ear to this leafy brigade,
In their verdant realm, there's never a trade.
For laughter and joy bloom like flowers in spring,
In this whimsical world where the green ones sing!

Roots in Stillness

Deep in the earth, where the shadows play,
Roots strike a pose, in the quiet ballet.
They tango and twist, in a dance underground,
While worms clap their hands, a strange sort of sound.

"Why so serious?" the roots rumbled low,
"Let's take a break, let's put on a show!"
They wiggled and giggled in endless delight,
Happiness grows in the stillness of night.

The soil whispers tales, of sun and of rain,
Of laughter that flows, like a soft gentle plane.
Together they ponder, in a quiet embrace,
Funny fables sprout in this snug little space.

So here's to the roots, in their secretive groove,
In silence they chatter, in their earthy move.
Let's cheer for the stillness, and the laughter it brings,
In the heart of the garden, where joy truly springs!

Requiem for a Withered Leaf

Ode to the leaf that fell with a sigh,
Once so vibrant, now waving goodbye.
Resting on soil, a final goodbye,
Did you forget that the sun was nigh?

Shade came shopping, a thief in the night,
Snatching vibrance, oh what a plight!
Now you're a snack for a hungry worm,
A feast for the soil, its newest term!

Oh leaf, we miss your emerald cheer,
Now you're just crispy, oh dear, oh dear!
Next time, my friend, stay close to the light,
Or face the fate of a leaf gone slight!

Thus ends the tale of a fluttering fate,
A snack for the soil, oh isn't it great?
We'll plant a new friend in your former space,
Hoping for a leaf with a better embrace!

Chronicles in a Terracotta Pot

In a pot so round, a world so small,
Lives a cactus named Spike, standing tall.
He brags to the daisies, 'I need no drink,'
While they sip sun tea, with time to think.

Next door is Fern, with a grand leafy gown,
Whispering secrets as she droops down.
'Water me, Spike, and I'll share a tale!'
But Spike just chuckles, 'You'll end up pale!'

Oh, the drama unfolds among pots every day,
With gossip of blooms that have gone astray.
Who's got the petals that catch the sun's rays?
And who's just pretending in a foggy haze?

In this terracotta realm, life's fluffy and bright,
Each plant with a story, a quirky delight.
So here's to the chronicles of greens and browns,
Let's sip on some soil, and toss out our frowns!

Ballad of the Blooming Bud

Oh little bud, perched up so high,
With colors so grand, you can't help but try.
You stretch in the sunlight, you dance with the breeze,
Proclaiming your charm with such wondrous ease.

In a world full of weeds, you stand proud and tall,
No worries of fading, you're having a ball.
The bees rush in close for a taste of your grin,
While you giggle and beam, let the pollination begin!

But the day will come when petals will fall,
You'll whisper sweet tales to the insects who call.
'Fear not, little friends, we shall spring back anew,'
For each blooming bud has a cycle that's true.

So raise your glass, dear friends, and don't shed a tear,
For the ballad of blooms is a song we all cheer.
From bud to blossom, the journey's a joy,
In the garden of life, every blossom's a ploy!

Lament of the Lonely Orchid

In a fancy pot, an orchid does weep,
Waiting for a friend, her level is deep.
With petals so glossy, she sighs with despair,
'Where's my friend Lily? I need someone there!'

She stares at the wall, decorated with snores,
While the spider plant dangles, just counting the spores.
'Oh, why must I bloom in this empty abode?'
With nobody near, her heart feels the load.

In dreams, she imagines a garden so bright,
With fellow flowers to dance through the night.
But alas, here she stands, a lone tragic star,
With a tale of lost blooms and a love gone too far!

So if you should find her, do stop for a chat,
Bring a friend from the garden, or just share your hat.
For an orchid needs company, it isn't too odd,
In the garden of dreams, we're all tied with a nod!

Resilience in Relics

In a pot with cracks and scars,
There lies a tale of sunshine and stars.
A cactus chuckles at the rain,
'You can't drown me, I'm here to remain!'

The rubber plant wears a crooked grin,
As dust bunnies dance, it lets them in.
'Let's throw a party, come join the fun!'
By the windowsill, we laugh in the sun.

A fern whispers secrets, green and bright,
'I've survived without much light!'
It winks at a flower that's a bit too bold,
'Watch me grow, if only I'm sold!'

In this quirky crew, the vibe's just right,
With every leaf, a newfound delight.
These relics of soil, so oddly arranged,
In their strange little world, life's never changed.

Stories Underneath the Clay

Beneath the surface, tales unfold,
Of roots that dance, both shy and bold.
Worms tell stories in a rhythmic hum,
'We keep it cozy, here's where we come!'

A potato whispers, 'I'm shaped like a lump,'
While the orchid scoffs, 'I've got style and jump!'
The beetroot boasts of its vibrant hue,
'In this earthy party, there's room for you!'

A rogue dandelion claims rightful ground,
'I'm a wish maker, spinning dreams around.'
With every bloom, they giggle and sway,
Creating legends in their own funky way.

So, here in the clay, life's a blend,
Of silly stories, on roots we depend.
Together they flourish, a quirky brigade,
In the heart of the pot, adventure is made.

Garden of Dreams

Where dreams sprout in pots of delight,
Sunshine whispers secrets, oh what a sight!
A basil plant thinks it's a chef so grand,
'I'll spice up your dinner, just lend me your hand!'

A minty mischievous rogue takes flight,
Twirling and swirling, oh what a delight!
'I'm the fresh air that dances in tea,
With every sip, you'll remember me!'

The marigold flaunts its bright golden crown,
'Paint the world sunny, brighten the town!'
While tiny violets giggle with glee,
'In this garden, we're wild and free!'

Together they blossom, a whimsical crew,
Turning plain pots into magic anew.
In this patch of laughter, each flower beams,
Creating a tapestry woven with dreams.

Soft Roots, Strong Lives

With roots so soft, yet strong as steel,
Potted dwellers whisper and squeal.
A timid sprout peeks out with fear,
'Will the sun really want me here?'

But the monstera shouts, 'Come join the scene!
In this pot, we're living our dream!'
They trade stories under the worn-down light,
'Every inch matters, oh what a sight!'

An ivy trails down, a cheeky delight,
'Hitch a ride on my leaves, we'll soar to new heights!'
While succulents giggle, basking in cheer,
'It's okay to stand out, there's no need for fear!'

So here they grow, in their quirky embrace,
Each pot a haven, a cozy place.
With roots entwined, and laughter at play,
They bloom in hilarity, come what may.

The Tangled Roots

In the corner, a pot sits tight,
With roots that spiral, oh what a sight!
They whisper secrets to the dirt below,
"We're not lost, just taking it slow!"

The leaves are gossiping, full of cheer,
"Is that a spider? Oh dear, oh dear!"
The sun spills laughter, so bright and warm,
While rain drops dance, causing quite a storm!

A cactus chimes in, pricked with pride,
"I'm tough and spiky, but don't run and hide!"
While succulents giggle in shades so bright,
"Don't mind our quirk, we're a colorful sight!"

Look at us grow, in this jolly pot,
Filled with antics, we love quite a lot!
In this little world, all's well and wise,
Join us in laughter, watch nature rise!

In a Blooming World

In the garden, colors swirl and sway,
Daisies tell stories in a fanciful way,
Lilies laugh loud, as butterflies roam,
"Off to the next flower, we'll make it our home!"

Petunias gossip with a sweet little grin,
"Who wore it best? Let's spin and spin!"
The sunflowers chuckle, tall and grand,
"Look up at us! We're the best in the land!"

A rose raises petals, feeling quite bold,
"Here comes the bee, I'm worth my weight in gold!"
While daffodils giggle with their golden hue,
"Just don't ask us for what we should do!"

With each blooming face, laughter unfolds,
In this whimsical patch, nature's treasure molds!
Join the jubilee, come frolic and play,
In this blooming world, we dance every day!

The Heartbeat of Nature

In every pot, a heartbeat sounds,
With every leaf, joy abounds.
A succulent winks, oh so sly,
"Bet you can't guess how old am I!"

The fern sways gently, doing a jig,
"A little water, not too big!"
While cacti snicker, spines held high,
"Life's all about where the sunniest spots lie!"

A tiny seedling peeks at the sky,
"Just wait till I get tall—I'll be spry!"
In this plant party, folks come and go,
With cheeky banter, entertaining the show!

So let's raise our pots, a toast to the sun,
Life's bloom is hilarious, and oh so fun!
In rustling leaves, hear laughter play,
In this heartbeat of nature, let joy stay!

A Botanical Reverie

In a cozy nook, where green friends reside,
A fern and a fig share tales side by side.
"Did you hear what the ivy said last night?
'Up the wall I'll climb, oh what a sight!'"

The basil dreams of flavors so fine,
"Just one pinch, and I'll make food divine!"
While the pothos slinks down with a wink,
"Watch me entwine; what do you think?"

The cactus rolls jokes, with a prickly flair,
"Why did the flower skip out? Too much care!"
And the geraniums blush at the tease,
"Let's keep our petals all smooth, if you please!"

In this botanical dream, smiles spread wide,
With giggles and grins, we dance with pride!
Here's to the fun in our leafy array,
In this verdant world, we'll laugh every day!

Poetry in Potting Soil

In a pot full of dirt, I found a rhyme,
Every worm a word, having a good time.
Seeds giggle softly, sprouting with glee,
Saying, "Plant us deeper; we long to be free!"

The sun beams down, casting shadows tall,
While leaves conspire to have a ball.
My cactus sings sweetly, thorns in a row,
"Don't touch my spines, or you'll reap what you sow!"

The gardener's trowel chips in with a jest,
Mixing up lyrics, forgetting the rest.
A little plant feels it's a strong poet,
But one tiny sunflower's sure to outgrow it.

So raise your pots high, let your laughter ring,
Talk to your flowers; let them dance and sing!
In this riot of growth, in clay and in toil,
They scribble their verses in potting soil.

Embers of a Bouncing Bamboo

Bamboo so bouncy, in a pot it leans,
Whispering secrets of tall leafy dreams.
"Don't ask me to keep still; I'm like a spring breeze,
When you dance with the wind, I do just as I please!"

A squirrel swings by, thinks it's a fine show,
Wonders if bamboo likes a good toe-to-toe.
Oh, how they giggle as branches entwine,
Caught in a game of pure plant-design!

But the ceramic pot rolls with a thud,
"Brace yourself, bamboo! You're headed for mud!"
Yet even in chaos, they laugh and they sway,
Sipping the sunlight on a bright rainy day.

So here's to our bamboo, both wild and carefree,
With roots deep in laughter, yearning to be free!
A comedy show, with nature's grand scheme,
Bouncing through life like a plant's funnest dream!

Variegated Dreams

In a variegated patch, colors collide,
Each leaf a surprise, a joy cannot hide.
The philodendron winks, while the fern does a twirl,
With laughter like bubbles that spiral and swirl.

"Who painted us different?" one leaf does inquire,
"Was it the gardener's brush, or did we conspire?"
"Perhaps we just wear our mishmash with pride,
A tapestry woven in green, side by side!"

Pot next door sulks, thinks it's all quite unfair;
"Why can't I be spotted, with ribbons to flair?"
Yet all plants agree that's not quite the way,
Every hue tells a story, in nature's ballet.

So skip to your pot, let the colors convene,
Each shade tells a story, in the bright light, we glean.
Variegation's a party where laughter's the scheme,
Roots wrapped together in variegated dreams!

Memoirs of the Maranta

Oh, Maranta, you lovely prayer plant,
With leaves that fold like a gossipy chant.
"Did you see the spider? Up there on the ledge!"
You plead for assistance, perched right on edge.

"Don't worry, dear friend, it's just a wee thing,
Let's talk about life, and the parties we bring!"
Your colors like watercolor, splashes of cheer,
In this leafy memoir, we'll shout far and near!

Every night you fold, a drama unfolds,
Chiding the moonlight who dares be too bold.
"Do respect my slumber; I need to recharge,
This life full of whispers, I'm living at large!"

So here's to the Maranta, full of delight,
In the realm of the plants, you shine ever bright.
Your funny escapades, in green, will endure,
In the memoirs of leaves, forever pure!

Lyrics of the Lush

In a bright green pot, a cactus sings,
Its prickly tunes are full of things.
With spines that twirl and leaves that laugh,
It tells a joke about the sun's warm staff.

A fern does a dance, a sway and a thrill,
With leaves that shimmer, it's quite the skill.
It bubbles and giggles in a sunny spot,
Winking at the snail who's moving slow, not a lot.

A succulent sits, so plump and round,
Busy keeping secrets, not making a sound.
When watered just right, it blooms with cheer,
But don't ask it why it's last in the beer.

The filmy ivy dreams of reaching heights,
Climbing curtains at the wildest flights.
With laughter alive in every green vine,
It says, "Join me, friend! This fun's divine!"

Reflections in a Rootball

In the muddy depths, a radish grins,
With a secret smile, it wiggles its fins.
"Dig me up!" it shouts, "come give me a try,
I promise I won't tell if you question why!"

Next to him, a potato rolls with glee,
In its jacket, it thinks, "I'm fancy, you see!"
With a wink and a nudge, it hums a new tune,
"Who needs a plate when you can dance by the moon?"

A pea pod swings, like it's part of a band,
With tiny green balls, just take it as planned.
Each time it pops, oh what a surprise!
"Let's party," it laughs, "with no need for ties!"

Among roots entwined, a clumsy old beet,
Trips over dreams, with unsteady feet.
But it chuckles and spins, like a top in the soil,
Saying, "Life's a garden—come join the toil!"

Melodies in the Moss

A patch of soft moss hums a sweet song,
Each tune like a hug, perfectly strong.
"It's cozy up here," the toadstool does croon,
"Let's have a gospel beneath the full moon!"

Tiny beetles join in, clapping their claws,
While the moss keeps swaying, without any flaws.
"Dance, little critters! Come join the fun,
With a bounce in your step, we'll be one by one!"

A ladybug twirls, dressed in dots and spots,
Singing to the starlight, pulling all the plots.
"Oh, what a night, with such lively cheer,
Let's rock this little patch, far and near!"

Under soft canopy, a party remains,
Nature's own laughter, with no signs of chains.
Together they weave a tapestry bright,
Of melodies whispered 'til morning light!

Tapestry of Tendrils

A vine stretches up, with quite the flair,
"Look at me reaching, I'm almost in the air!"
With tendrils that twist and shimmy with pride,
It yells, "Hey, sunlight! Come take a ride!"

Next to it, a clumsy sprout stumbles about,
With leaves that flop, and an uncertain shout.
"Do I go left, or am I all turned around?
All of this growing? It's chaos I've found!"

A creeping charlie giggles, covered in dust,
It whispers, "My friend, you simply must trust.
With a wiggle and jiggle, we'll find our own way,
Tomorrow brings sunshine, we'll laugh as we sway!"

In this green circus, all plants play a part,
With jokes and with jests, and a whole lot of heart.
From roots to the leaves, let's giggle and twirl,
We're the funniest friends, in this potted world!

www.ingramcontent.com/pod-product-compliance
Lightning Source LLC
Chambersburg PA
CBHW070329120526
44590CB00017B/2843